The Narcissist's Secret

Why They Hate You (and What to Do About It)

Dan Desmarques

22 Lions

The Narcissist's Secret: Why They Hate You (and What to Do About It)

Written by Dan Desmarques

Contents

Introduction

In a world where interpersonal relationships are becoming increasingly complex, understanding the intricacies of human behavior has never been more important. This book, The Narcissist's Secret: Why They Hate You (and What to Do About It), delves deep into the enigmatic world of narcissism, shedding light on the hidden motivations, destructive patterns, and profound impact of narcissistic individuals on those around them.

As we navigate the maze of modern society, we often encounter individuals who seem to operate on a different wavelength-those who exude an air of superiority, manipulate others with ease, and leave a trail of emotional devastation in their wake. These are the narcissists among us, and their presence can be felt in our personal relationships, in the workplace, and even in the highest echelons of power.

This book aims to unravel the complex tapestry of narcissistic behavior, offering readers a comprehensive understanding of why narcissists act the way they do, how they affect those around them, and, most importantly, how to protect oneself from their toxic influence. Drawing on extensive research, clinical observation, and real-life experience, we explore the multifaceted nature of narcissism, from its roots in childhood trauma to its manifestation in adult relationships.

In these pages, we will examine the various facets of Narcissistic Personality Disorder, including its classification within Cluster B personality disorders, its neurobiological underpinnings, and its societal implications. We will delve into the inner world of the narcissist, uncovering the deep-seated insecurities and fears that drive their behavior, and explore how these manifest in their interactions with others. But this book isn't just about understanding narcissists - it's about empowering those affected by their behavior.

The book offers practical strategies for identifying narcissistic traits, setting boundaries, and protecting yourself from manipulation and abuse. We will also explore the journey of healing for those who have been victims of narcissistic abuse, offering guidance on rebuilding self-esteem and reclaiming a sense of self.

As we embark on this journey of discovery, it's important to note that the term "narcissist" is not used lightly or as a catch-all term for difficult personalities. Instead, we approach this topic with nuance and depth, recognizing the spectrum of narcissistic traits and the complex interplay of factors that contribute to their development.

Whether you're a mental health professional seeking to deepen your understanding of narcissistic personality disorder, someone who suspects you may be in a relationship with a narcissist, or simply an individual interested in human psychology, this book offers valuable insights and practical tools for navigating the challenging terrain of narcissistic relationships.

By the end of this book, readers will not only have a clearer understanding of narcissistic behavior, but will also be equipped with the knowledge and strategies necessary to protect themselves and thrive in a world where narcissism seems to be on the rise. Let us begin this journey of understanding, healing, and empowerment together.

Chapter 1: Covert Hostility

When narcissists perceive that their image is being threatened by someone else's decision, they will do whatever they can to turn the situation around and make the other person look like the one in the wrong. This can include provoking the other person and then secretly filming their reactions, and even editing the result to make it look like the other person has mental problems and is dangerous for no logical reason. Reporters do this all the time because they are experts at fabricating news when there is nothing to say. But narcissists are more likely to do this when they perceive danger in the near future, which is why you should never give information to a narcissist. They will distort it and use it against you.

Note that they perceive everything as a threat, even friendly warnings, and will take revenge based on that perception alone. It is not uncommon for a narcissist to hate the person who tried to help them the most, because they perceive help as hidden hostility and use it against others. They project their own manipulative intentions onto those who are genuinely trying to help them. Another thing they do is perceive a threat in their environment as competition, and then do their best to make sure the other person ends up fired or in jail. They may do this by spreading rumors that make others hate the person.

Often, however, the threat comes from a spouse who has more credibility among family members, or a friend who is wiser and able to distinguish lies from the truth. Even a student who is capable of asking the right questions is perceived as a threat by professors who don't want others to know about their facade, their manipulations, and their absolute ignorance in doing their job. For example, I was hated immensely as a student for no other reason than asking the right questions instead of accepting everything that was said in the classroom like others. These professors often slandered me in their conversations, as I was told by some of them, because they were obsessed with their hatred for me.

It took me years to understand why, because I was just a student asking what I thought were normal questions. Later I realized that such people actively work to undermine or sabotage a person's social image with the goal of getting them removed from their position or discredited, which in this case means trying to make them fail and get them expelled. That is why I was never allowed to see my exam papers after they were graded. They would hide them and only show me the final grade. When I protested the situation through legal means, they used my response to slander me even more to others.

They intensified their efforts to have me expelled when I asked for justice. They spread more false stories and rumors about me because I was perceived as a threat, and they turned others against me so that no one would listen to me. Were they right? Somehow they were, because I exposed them. I never tolerated their abuse and even confronted them when others were too afraid to say what they thought, although they secretly thanked me for being their voice.

I was punished for being honest, selfless, courageous, just, and for representing the needs of other students to be heard. I never said anything that others couldn't see, but they were too afraid to speak up.

This is exactly how narcissists always win, by making an example of the scapegoat while keeping everyone else afraid that they will be next. They can't burn you alive in the public square these days, so they humiliate you. The intent is the same, to burn your integrity in the public square.

There is nothing reasonable to do with these people except to throw them out of all institutions. They are parasites and demons at best, and cannot be compared to or treated as ordinary people. The credibility they gain as professors and therapists means nothing because they do not really apply any science or integrity to their work.

Chapter 2: Effects of Low Energy Frequencies

I once confronted a psychologist who encouraged her patient to use drugs, both psychotropic and psychoactive, ignoring the fact that this person was having suicidal thoughts. She even told the patient that it was normal to think about suicide, ignoring the danger the patient was in. Instead of talking to me about her use of psychology to psychologically abuse someone, she ran away from me. I called her a psychopath who should be internalized in a psychiatric institution instead of getting money from others while abusing them in therapy, but she reacted like a child and just ran away from me.

This was in Lithuania, which, according to the World Health Organization (WHO), often tops the list in terms of suicide rates per 100,000 people. Lithuania is also usually among the top 5 countries in the world for suicide. But while people try to guess the causes, they're right in front of everyone: Their own psychologists. This one in particular writes for magazines, has a blog and even coaches other psychologists in their work. It sounds too surreal to be true, but it is much more common than people want to believe.

Although the Lithuanians themselves are some of the dirtiest, rudest and stupidest people I have ever met, their therapists make the already degrading culture much worse than it is. The only reason anyone would want to travel to Lithuania is to visit the world's largest open-air museum of narcissism: Their culture. Here you can see people belittling each other, making the stupidest assumptions about everyone, judging all the time, gossiping negatively about others for no particular reason except envy and a delusional sense of arrogance, and worse, putting glass and rocks in soup, making pizzas with rotten cheese and rotten mushrooms, making sushi with rotten rice, even mold on the rice, and reusing coffee cups that have never been washed. It is a complete display of filth and hypocrisy, but it is also the most obvious demonstration of narcissism when it is ingrained in a culture.

They will tell you that the glass or rock you found in the food was an accident, as if it didn't happen all the time and on purpose, when they hate their customers and even speak rudely to them. They will deny that they don't wash their cups and plates, even though I have seen it with my own eyes. They will also tell you that people didn't stare at you aggressively, but were too shy to speak to you. These reactions are also part of what narcissists do when you ask for an explanation. It is called denying your own reality so that you think you are the crazy one, not them.

Although I think Lithuania and Poland could compete for first place in racism, xenophobia, and ignorance, Lithuanians are especially antagonistic in the sense that they bump into the people they hate, especially travelers who look different from the locals. They also judge people by the color of their skin and won't even change their path if a black person is walking in the same direction on the street. Worse, if you are a black person, strangers on the street will tell the white people next to you in their own language to be careful and avoid you.

Talking about Lithuania and Poland is like talking about Stupidland and Naziland, because they are exactly and proudly what their history and modern statistics say about them. The only exceptions I found in these countries came from their immigrants. But taken together, these two nations could represent the United States of Narcissism.

Although some nations have more mentally ill people than others, often because of cultures that promote mental illness, you must know that what we call toxic people, oppressive people, stupid people, psychopaths, sociopaths, or simply narcissists, among other Cluster B personality disorders, as classified by the Diagnostic and Statistical Manual of Mental Disorders (DSM-5) published by the American Psychiatric Association, refer to individuals who express a certain state of mind within a certain vibration that is common to them.

This isn't just theory or opinion because it can be measured and you can feel when someone in the room has a higher vibration than you. This altered frequency in the energy field is perceived as a threat to them, even if that person has never opened their mouth to speak or is simply a stranger alone.

I've seen this happen to others and myself countless times, including people turning their faces in my direction when I wasn't near or in front of them, or running away from me in fear, just because they sensed danger when I was sitting alone on a bench in a park or coffee shop, and doing nothing to justify such behavior.

Chapter 3: The Invisible Battle

Many people react in very schizophrenic ways when I am around for no other reason than how they feel because their energy frequency is extremely low. I remember once walking on the island of Chios in Greece and seeing a woman dressed all in black sitting on a bench overlooking the sea. She sensed my presence and immediately turned her head in my direction in fear. When she saw me, she got up and started running in the opposite direction, looking back to see if I was following her. But I was just an ordinary person dressed like a local and minding my own business. I was just walking by myself and would pass her without saying anything if she kept sitting on the same bench. Her paranoid reaction made no sense at all, except when you look at the explanation of energy frequencies. She had a negative energy field and my presence, even at a distance, triggered her insecurities.

I was not surprised because this happens to me all the time. But I don't expect the average person to understand this because the average person is blind to this information. However, I was curious about students who claimed to feel more energetic, motivated, and happy in my presence for no particular reason. They showed me that if someone is predisposed to a higher frequency, they will naturally absorb it and benefit from it instead of being afraid of it. If this doesn't happen, there is fear and anxiety in the mind of the narcissist, who may plot a way to remove the higher frequency individual from that environment through slander.

In one particular case, one of my colleagues from the United States was caught listening to my class from behind the door to gather information he could use against me.

Those who see these things and can't understand them tend to rationalize the behavior to avoid confronting the reality in front of them because it escapes their perception of the world. It is so out of the realm of reality for the vast majority of people that they refuse to believe it when it is happening in front of their eyes. The people around me would try to come up with reasons where there were none valid enough to replace the fact that I was being targeted for no other reason than my vibration. The attacker himself will often rationalize the reasons why he hates me, because he has none that he can verbalize, and that is why he provokes and insults first. They try to get that reason.

These things happened so often in my life that I felt hopeless, like I was going crazy from so many constant attacks, while the whole rest of society would deny the facts even when they witnessed them with their own eyes. I had to come to the conclusion that the average person denies seeing what they cannot understand, thus refusing to believe their eyes when they have no explanation in their minds for what they see. As a result, I was only able to understand these situations by immersing myself in various religious subjects. It was through various experts in secret knowledge and exorcism that I finally got the answers. Still, I could not understand why they were targeting me, and it took me much longer to see it because I was trained by two narcissistic parents to never see these things.

It was only when I opened up to my true potential as a spirit that it all came to light. Now I expect these things to happen because of the importance of my work in the world and my renewed confidence in my abilities. So instead of fighting the nature of evil, I have learned to accept it as simply the state of the world. Many are blind, others are pure evil, and where the light goes, the darkness reacts with discomfort.

Being trained in the art of telepathy took my knowledge to a whole new depth, for I never imagined how incredibly disgusting and filthy the mind of a narcissist could be. Being able to read my mother's mind and redirect and even nullify her thoughts made me realize how obsessed she was with belittling and invalidating me, as if she could not control her need to attack me and was tormented by it. I would see the exact same thing in narcissistic partners who shed tears when the relationship ended as a result of their own negative compulsive behaviors.

Narcissists are not only mentally ill, they are vessels for demonic influence of the lowest nature. Society does not have the knowledge or discernment to deal with such individuals, and psychiatry is far from truly understanding them beyond their actions. In fact, the apathetic state of the masses leads them to deny the evidence in front of their eyes and dismiss the negative influence of narcissism as justifiable when it comes to finding a scapegoat to avoid looking at themselves and addressing the dangers posed by the narcissists around them.

Chapter 4: The Contradictions of the Narcissistic Mind

Although society erroneously assumes that the best response to evil people is to give them no reason, the truth is that as long as your vibration is high enough, you will be targeted by these low-vibrational people who often act as vessels for demonic entities precisely because their soul is deprived of life energy and their vibration is low enough to attract such entities. They have lowered their vibration by choice, by committing crimes they don't want others to know about, by using mind-altering drugs, and by feeding themselves resentful thoughts about others, even if the cause is a parent who traumatized them for life, or simply jealousy.

It is not uncommon for a woman who was abandoned by her father or saw her father physically abuse her mother as a child to become a narcissist who forever hates men and distrusts women, or even harbors resentment against women while pretending to help them. This was the case with a Ukrainian woman I met who was abandoned by her father as a child and then decided to work as a psychologist helping women through divorce. She also admitted that she could not solve anyone's problems.

I have met many psychologists who do just that, but with each act against society, such an individual perpetuates his mental state and goes deeper into the abyss of fear where he can only find peace by manipulating, belittling and degrading others. This is why so many of these people suffer terribly with their own minds and constantly seek relief in alternative methods, as was the case with that Ukrainian psychologist who constantly sought answers and found none. She herself was lonely and unable to find a partner at the age of 35.

It seemed she was looking for answers as much as she was looking for justification for her beliefs, because that's the cycle narcissists put themselves in when they refuse to move beyond the rationalizations they make of the world. A narcissist can insult you a thousand times and then, when you respond, say: "See, I knew you were pretending to be someone else because you are not a nice person."

They see others as they see themselves, so they don't believe anyone can pretend to be someone else for that long. In other words, they can't believe that people can be honest, because in the narcissist's brain, one equals two and equals zero. Or as my narcissistic mother used to tell me: People are evil and you have to learn to be smarter than them.

This is really how narcissists see themselves in the world, as victims of a greater evil, where their own evil is justified by the need to survive in such a hell. This is why they think morality is for the weak and honesty is for the stupid. They value only deception, which is why Narcissists' favorite movies are often listed as The Shawshank Redemption, Basic Instinct, The Talented Mr. Ripley, Nymphomaniac, The Wolf of Wall Street, and Ex Machina. What do these movies have in common? Individuals who succeed by deception and fool everyone.

Narcissists study themselves through movies as much as they study the occult, not because the occult is evil in itself, but because they are looking for ways to get information about other people that has never been told. A narcissist almost never reflects on his behavior, even when he wants to, which is why he ends up going deeper in his manipulation when he studies himself. The only reason a narcissist would go to a therapist would be to learn more about his own victims. Almost every narcissist has a deck of tarot cards hidden somewhere, not to study himself, but to study the people he knows.

For the same reasons, it is not uncommon for many failed psychologists suffering from narcissism to explore the use of cartomancy, runes, and other divinatory methods in their practice with the intention of healing themselves and others, essentially acknowledging the failure of psychology to help them. But just as narcissists seek therapy to improve their tactics, narcissistic therapists offer their patients their absolute failure through more manipulative methods and further degradation of society, which they present as innovative forms of uplifting others based on occult practices and studies.

They do the same through religion, which is why it can be so confusing to find rapists and pedophiles among religious leaders. In the early 2000s, the Archdiocese of Boston was at the center of a major scandal involving the sexual abuse of minors by priests. The investigation revealed that the church had systematically covered up these abuses for decades. John Geoghan, a Catholic priest in the Archdiocese of Boston, was accused of sexually abusing more than 130 children over a 30-year period. But stories of pedophilia and rape are also found among Hindu gurus, Islamic scholars, Buddhist monks, Sikh officials and Jewish rabbis.

Chapter 5: The Devolution of Thought

There is no end to what narcissists can do, as I have seen many times over the years. They even write books on alternative methods or invent their own and give them mystical names like cosmic connections and then use the title of psychologist or doctor to give more credibility to their destruction, when the act itself is a complete contradiction of what science is supposed to be.

Not surprisingly, these are the same people who confuse the brain with the soul and spirit, mixing them together as if they were making a smoothie out of different ingredients.

On the other hand, the brain is not compartmentalized as neurology teaches, often contradicting itself in its own theories, but rather acts as an integrative machine that operates based on the spiritual state of the individual, and this means that if the individual shifts his focus to negativity, resentment, and self-deprecation, these emotions will act as catalysts for the brain and it will shift accordingly.

Confusing the whole brain with its parts, or the brain with the soul, personality, and spirit, is the root cause of all misunderstandings in both science and religion, and not surprisingly, narcissists are the ones who perpetuate, promote, and reinforce such confusion the most. But if the narcissist's favorite weapon is confusion, the opposite is also what narcissists fear most: Clarity, insight, and objectivity.

The more you understand and know, the more you can resist the chaos narcissists promote and distance yourself from such a world. So what do narcissists do to stop curious minds like yours? They write the books that promise answers and add more confusion to your mind. They also replace your need to understand with the imperative to memorize or face punishment through the educational system or whatever method of learning you are going through.

In essence, narcissists do their best to keep you from understanding anything, and with so many of them in the world, it is not surprising that trust, or the ability to be trusted, has become such a rare quality. Yet even this is attacked by narcissists as they do their best to discredit the most trustworthy person. Narcissists do this all the time when they review my books, leaving insults that say nothing about the content. The author is evil, crazy, narcissistic, and psychopathic are among such insults.

The narcissists often win because the rest of the population is stupid enough, apathetic enough, and misinformed enough to believe anything, or at least consider a foolish opinion without any common sense. Many people will never find the answers they are looking for because a narcissist wrote a lie about an author or his book.

What a shame that people are so easily fooled. Ignorance is truly their undoing in many more ways than those perceived by the eyes. But the world will not be a better place if we allow this dynamic to continue. Narcissists are much more active in destroying the world than other people are in praising those who help them and contribute to a better world. A narcissist will invest billions to destroy a nation, but the average person will rarely pay anything for a book.

According to a 2018 Pew Research Center survey in the United States, about 24% of American adults said they had not read any books, but in the same year, the United States invested $740 billion in military activities.

You are a fool if you think that narcissists will ever change this dynamic and not work harder to make it worse. Narcissists are not interested in educating a population. They are interested in gaining more power through the downfall and impoverishment of others, so that is where they invest their time and effort.

People are victims of their own stupidity when they invest their time in fighting other groups of people instead of reading, but the average idiot is more likely to pick up a gun to shoot someone with any excuse in his head than to pick up a book to learn something new.

If people spent more time reading, they would spend less time judging and gossiping about others. The person who is preoccupied with judging others certainly has nothing to occupy his mind with, for it is impossible to listen to an audio book and remain focused on what other people are doing around us.

Chapter 6: Why Narcissists Stay the Same

Narcissists are predictable by any psychiatric diagnosis, precisely because therapists do not address the causes, but simply make people comfortable with the effects, often teaching them that they are merely an effect of the illness of others and that there is nothing they can do about it. Or worse, they use mystical methods to teach them that being such an effect is their life's path, thus degrading them through the use of false teachings.

To change his situation, the individual needs to reform his entire state of being, which in most cases will never happen, precisely because he has attached himself to this artificial personality and is afraid of losing it and becoming nothing, starting all over again to learn how to be human. Evil people take advantage of this reality when they use it against the person to claim that he is on a spiritual path, because then they can profit more from that belief, while suppressing the individual's insecurity behind their false confidence or absolute trust in a false theory.

This is the same tactic that many preachers use and why it is so effective. They prey on the fact that people want to be loved and accepted, not changed and judged. I know this because whenever I have been able to help such people, this is exactly what they have told me: "I don't know who I am anymore, and I'm afraid."

This state wouldn't last long because no one wants to be afraid of the unknown, even if that unknown is an imaginary boundary in the mind. As a result, they quickly seek anchors of validation that root them back into the old self. This means seeking out companions and peers who will help them, either by causing them to hate the one who is trying to help them, or simply by distracting the narcissist with drugs and convincing them to make mistakes that damage the therapy they are receiving. They keep regressing to the old state until they finally stop changing out of exhaustion. That is why they cannot be changed.

Society as a whole will go to great lengths to prevent them from changing, as if a legion of demons would come to their aid to prevent them from ever seeing the light. The worst people you meet are often what the narcissist calls his best friends, because the narcissist is an underdeveloped child, an idiot in an adult body. They would rather die stupid than change, convinced that it is better to die as what others approve of them than to be alone in the bliss of happiness. They don't even believe that such a thing exists, so they laugh at any spiritual teaching that shows a path to a higher self and constantly belittle those who follow spiritual paths. Many of them claim that I am making up what I write because they do not believe and even hate the idea that this information could help anyone.

They are averse to helping themselves and others, so they hate those who provide effective help. If the narcissist becomes a professional in a field that is supposed to help others, they will pervert the information and the process. This is why doctors murder patients all the time under the guise of misdiagnosis, why parents send their children to schools where they are bullied and beaten or even killed in fights and robberies, and why professors deliberately lie with statistics to push their own social agenda on students.

We could argue whether such people are really stupid, just arrogant, or evil. Often they are all three, while other times they are clearly evil and just seem stupid. In any case, they are determined to succeed at short-term goals or tasks that produce quick and visible results rather than thinking long-term, which is why they focus on stopping others rather than planning for the future or seeking agreements. Their backbiting is essentially an attempt to stop someone who is a threat to them, even if that threat is imaginary. They are determined to stop society and set it back for the same reason, because putting others down makes them feel safer within themselves.

One of the reasons they win at this game is because they know that most people are selfish, so the narcissist can exploit their needs through that selfishness and then gain their trust, especially if those people are friends of the one they are trying to target. For example, a narcissistic nurse may offer to help a relative with health problems and then use the situation to slander someone she hates, and she will do this carefully after gaining the trust of the sick person who now feels indebted to the nurse.

They use the same tactic to climb the social ladder, because they're not very good at gaining people's trust through their work, because it's basically a sham. Instead, they sabotage the image of others to gain the upper hand, and they do this after carefully studying them and copying their best traits to pretend to be superior.

Chapter 7: When Good Deeds Go Unreturned

You will know who your enemies are, and especially who has betrayed your trust, when you need help and everyone abandons you, including the people you have helped, whether it was to get a job or to overcome loneliness and financial difficulties. Besides narcissists, stupid people in general have short memories, so they don't really have any empathy or sense of responsibility towards those who help them. One moment they ask for your help, and an hour later, when you call and ask for it, they say: Good luck!

I have helped people start a business who did not even offer me a couch to sleep on and that tells you a lot about the level of selfishness in people, either you have known them for many years or they are family members. The stench of garbage is the same, so I have removed all people I can't trust from my life.

It's sad to think that you can't really trust most people because they're worthless. But it's not even useful to help them because they betray you.

Once one of my readers asked to work for me, and I said I needed someone to help me translate the books. She asked for $5,000 up front, and when she saw the amount of work, she said she wouldn't do it. Would she give me the money back if I paid her? Probably not! But then what is the point of my books if readers try to cheat their own favorite author? What is their moral level? Why should I even write a book in such a world?

When I use the term stupid people, I could say morons, toxic individuals, narcissists, sociopaths, or psychopaths, but the word itself doesn't really matter, because there is not enough clarity on the planet yet to understand the meaning and extension of what I am trying to say, which is that there is a large population on this planet that does not deserve anything they get, not even sympathy for their misfortune. There are as many narcissists with power as there are people who disrespect and abuse those who help them. The involvement of one element in causing evil is just as bad as the other.

We cannot imagine a better world with advanced technology without considering the need for more honesty, integrity, altruism, kindness, empathy, creativity and trustworthiness in society. The advancement in comfort and efficiency of systems and institutions in the world will never exist without the advancement of human qualities.

If you allow the narcissists to win, you will pay the price in self-inflicted karma - the problems in your daily life. For there will never be more entrepreneurship, more ideas and better science, or even more honesty and a higher level of commitment to the common good, regardless of race or creed or color, if the narcissists continue to suppress these things and degrade the most important, hardworking and innovative people among us. This will never happen as long as narcissists are allowed to drag everyone backwards, degrade human values, corrupt the law, and degrade morality while occupying positions of moral superiority and power.

Narcissists are hostile to those with the most potential and often degrade a person's sense of self. If you are a child, the effects can last a long time. For example, I remember my parents telling me what a useless person I was because I couldn't cook, but they never taught me, and they never asked anyone to teach me. Instead, they were happy to use the fact that they had to feed me to humiliate me, and this was one of the many tactics they used to psychologically abuse me. Later in life I learned to cook for myself, and I am proud to say that I cook better than many of the restaurants I eat in around the world, but I have no motivation to cook for myself, and maybe I never will. Unless I am cooking for others, I have no interest in eating what I cook. My parents destroyed that joy forever.

When you grow up in a toxic environment, especially when you are surrounded by idiots everywhere you go, it can take years to understand what really happened to you. Most people will not even allow you to do that because they are so incredibly stupid that they will assume that such stories are made up or that you somehow deserve what happened to you.

Many people have committed suicide for much less, but rarely if ever do their killers go to jail because psychological abuse is not as obvious a crime as stabbing someone. It can be more destructive, however, not only when it involves suicide, but because the effects last a lifetime and the impact is much greater than a physical wound - it means losing everyone you knew, including yourself and what made you happy, and having to start your life over again, many times if necessary.

Meanwhile, you have a target on your back that says you are a victim. You act like a victim, you think like a victim, and you may not even know it, simply because you spent your entire childhood afraid of the consequences of your thoughts and ashamed to be alive.

Chapter 8: Confronting Narcissistic Lies

One of the reasons that narcissists and empaths can be easily confused is that both are chasing love, the love they never had. The difference is that the empath seeks validation through her actions, while the narcissist seeks validation through her lies.

Very few people can tell the difference, which is why the narcissist often wins. The narcissist wins in the short term because he is able to fool many, but in the long term we know that hard work and dedication to life always wins because it builds character and leads to more experiences and also more opportunities in life.

The impression that the empath loses is an illusion, because it has to do with the people he has to leave behind when he finds his own way, people who have left him in favor of the narcissist. The empath can only lose if he forgets himself, which is what the narcissist intends when he lowers his self-esteem. The empath also loses if he is afraid of offending other people and avoids disagreeing with them, or if he develops an irrational fear of success for these reasons. It can also happen if he has an irrational fear of punishment.

Just as narcissists are experts at undermining other people's potential for success, empaths become experts at undermining their own potential, often downgrading themselves when their life accomplishments show the opposite. We mistake the empath's behavior for humility instead of seeing it for what it really is: self-abasement, self-denigration, self-deprecation, and self-devaluation.

The empath may also be confusing himself when he thinks he is being humble, but his feelings about himself and his thoughts are very clear and self-explanatory:

- Self-deprecation is an extreme form of self-abasement, usually driven by feelings of guilt, shame, or worthlessness. Example: "I'm a complete failure, I can't do anything right, I'm worthless."

- Self-denigration involves both putting oneself down and diminishing one's worth. It can be used in a broader sense to include both self-abasement and self-deprecation. It often involves a negative self-image and a tendency to belittle one's abilities or accomplishments.

Example: "I always screw things up. I'm not smart enough for this job. I'm just not cut out for success."

- Self-deprecation involves making disparaging or belittling remarks about oneself, often in a humorous or self-mocking way. It can be a way to deflect criticism, appear humble, or make others feel more comfortable. However, it can also be a sign of low self-esteem when taken to extremes. Example: "Oh, I'm just a terrible cook. You really shouldn't expect much from my cooking.

- Self-devaluation involves undervaluing or underestimating one's abilities, worth, or contributions. It often stems from a lack of confidence or self-esteem and can lead to a failure to recognize or acknowledge one's own strengths and accomplishments. Example: "I don't think I'm qualified for this promotion. There are so many people who are better than me."

Each of these terms captures a different nuance of how empaths might put themselves down or underestimate their worth. But to understand why the empath has internalized such feelings and thoughts about himself, we must consider what he heard in his childhood that caused them. Some examples of common narcissistic phrases are

- "You're always so sensitive. You need to toughen up."

- "You're not as special as you think you are. You're just like everyone else."

- "You're not capable of handling this. You should step aside and let someone more competent take over."

- "You're not as good as you think you are. You're just average."

- "You're not worth the effort. You should just give up."

These statements are designed to undermine the empath's self-esteem and confidence, causing him to question his abilities and worth. The narcissist uses these tactics to maintain control and superiority, often causing the empath to internalize feelings of inadequacy and self-doubt.

Chapter 9: Countering Narcissistic Manipulation

Consider the examples of narcissistic phrases below and use them to identify past or present narcissists in your life. Begin your healing journey by affirming the opposite of what you have heard.

A) Countering Self-abasement - This category focuses on phrases that diminish one's worth and happiness:

A.1. I am worthy of love and the good things in life. I deserve happiness and success.

Counter: You're worthless. You don't deserve anything good in life.

A.2. I am on a path of growth and success. I will achieve great things.

Counter: You're a complete failure. You'll never amount to anything.

A.3. I am doing my best and making progress. I am not a disappointment.

Counter: You are a disappointment. You always disappoint everyone.

A.4. I am important and my feelings matter. I deserve to be treated with respect.

Counter: Your feelings don't matter. They're not important enough to worry about.

A.5. I have the power to make positive changes in my life. I am capable of achieving my goals.

Counter: You can't change anything. You just don't have the ability to achieve your goals.

B) Countering Self-Denigration - This category includes phrases that belittle one's intelligence, abilities, and potential:

B.1. I am intelligent and capable. I can handle any challenge that comes my way.

Counter: You're not smart enough to handle it. Let someone else do it.

B.2. I am destined for success. I will not accept limitations placed on me by others.

Counter: You're not destined for success. You should simply accept your limitations.

B.3. I am capable of learning and improving. I am not defined by my past mistakes.

Counter: You're just not good enough. You should give up.

B.4. I have unique insights and ideas that are valuable. I am creative and resourceful.

Counter: Your ideas are stupid. You're not creative or resourceful.

B.5. I can learn new things and adapt to change. I welcome growth and challenges.

Counter: You can't learn new things. You'll never be able to adapt or change.

C) Countering Self-deprecation - This category includes phrases that minimize or ridicule one's abilities and competencies:

C.1. I am a good cook and competent in the kitchen. I expect great things from my cooking.

Counter: Oh, you're just a terrible cook. You really shouldn't expect much from your cooking.

C.2. I am skilled and capable. I am good at this task.

Counter: You're not very good at it. Maybe you should stick to simpler tasks.

C.3. I am competent and reliable. I can handle this responsibility.

Counter: You're not reliable enough to handle this. You should leave it to someone more capable.

C.4. I communicate well and express my thoughts effectively. I am confident in my abilities.

Counter: You're terrible at expressing yourself. You should just keep quiet.

C.5. I am organized and efficient. I manage my time and responsibilities well.

Counter: You're so disorganized. You can't handle any responsibility.

D) Countering Self-Devaluation - This category includes phrases that dismiss or undervalue one's talents, contributions, and assets:

D.1. I am talented and capable. I am realistic about my abilities and strengths.

Counter: You're not as talented as you think you are. You need to be more realistic about your abilities.

D.2. I make a significant contribution to my team and projects. My input is valuable.

Counter: You don't contribute much. You should let others take the lead.

D.3. I am valuable and my input is valued. I am an asset to my team.

Counter: You don't contribute enough. You should step aside.

D.4. My efforts are recognized and valued. I make a difference in my work.

Counter: Nobody cares about your efforts. You don't really make a difference.

D.5. I bring unique strengths and perspectives to my team. My input is essential.

Counter: Your strengths are irrelevant. Your input isn't needed or wanted.

Chapter 10: Identifying Trigger Phrases

While the previous sections focused on directly countering narcissistic phrases, trigger phrases are more subtle and insidious. These phrases are designed to elicit specific emotional responses and manipulate the victim's perceptions and feelings.

Trigger phrases are often used to gaslight, blame, or dismiss the victim's experiences, creating self-doubt and confusion. Understanding and recognizing these triggers is critical for victims to counter the manipulative tactics and reaffirm their reality and self-worth.

In the examples below you will find the following:

1 - Phrases used by the narcissist and their purpose.

2 - Triggers: The intended immediate emotional or psychological response to the phrase. If used often, it becomes a conditioned response. In other words, it causes you to involuntarily feel a certain way and has predetermined physiological and

psychological effects that can be interpreted as a trauma response. This is why victims of narcissistic abuse may show symptoms of post-traumatic stress disorder even after the narcissist is gone.

3 - Effects: The long-term impact on the victim's behavior, self-image, or relationship dynamics. In this case, we are talking about the psychological damage that affects victims of narcissism for the rest of their lives if not confronted and dealt with. These effects are also at the heart of the mistakes victims make in response to their experiences.

A) Phrases designed to challenge reality and perception - These phrases are designed to distort the victim's sense of reality and cause them to question their memories, perceptions, and emotional responses:

1. "You're crazy" and "You're overreacting";

Triggers: Causes the victim to doubt his or her sanity, perceptions, and emotional reactions.

Intended Effect: Causes the victim to question their reality and suppress their feelings, leading to self-doubt and confusion.

2. "I never said that" and "I never did that";

Trigger: Causes the victim to question their memory and perception of events.

Intended Effect: Causes self-doubt, confusion, and makes the victim unsure of their recollection of facts, ultimately devaluing their experiences.

3. "You're hypersensitive";

Trigger: Dismisses and invalidates the victim's feelings and emotions.

Intended Effect: Makes the victim feel oversensitive, causing them to suppress or ignore their feelings and needs. This may also cause the victim to doubt their emotional intelligence and resilience.

4. "You made me do it";

Trigger: Blames the victim for the manipulator's actions, shifting responsibility to the victim.

Intended Effect: Causes the victim to feel guilty, responsible, and at fault for the manipulator's behavior. This can lead to self-blame, self-doubt, and a distorted sense of responsibility.

B) Phrases designed to make the victim feel bad about him/herself - These phrases are designed to lower the victim's self-esteem and make him/her feel inadequate or unlovable:

1. "You're selfish" and "You only care about yourself";

Triggers: Accusing the victim of being self-centered and inconsiderate.

Intended Effect: Makes the victim feel guilty for having needs and wanting to put herself first. This can lead to self-neglect and a distorted sense of priorities.

2."No one else would put up with you."

Trigger: Implies that the victim is difficult to love or be around.

Intended Effect: Makes the victim feel inadequate, unlovable, and trapped in the relationship. This can lead to feelings of helplessness and low self-esteem.

3. "I'm sorry you feel this way";

Trigger: Dismisses the victim's feelings without taking responsibility.

Intended Effect: Dismisses the victim's feelings and shifts the focus away from the manipulator's actions. This can cause the victim to repress their feelings and doubt their emotional experiences.

4. "You're imagining things";

Trigger: Gaslights the victim, causing them to doubt their perceptions.

Intended Effect: Causes self-doubt, confusion, and makes the victim unsure of their interpretation of events. This can lead to a distorted sense of reality and self-questioning.

C) Phrases designed to make the victim feel guilty, ungrateful, or dramatic - These phrases are designed to manipulate the victim into feeling guilty, blameworthy, or exaggerating their feelings:

1. "You should be grateful for what I do for you."

Triggers: Implies that the victim is ungrateful for the manipulator's efforts.

Intended Effect: Makes the victim feel ungrateful and indebted, encouraging them to tolerate poor treatment or abuse. This can lead to a sense of obligation and entrapment.

2. "You're just like your mother", "You're just like your father", or "You're just like your uncle";

Trigger: Compares the victim to a family member, often with negative connotations.

Intended Effect: Provokes negative emotions and makes the victim feel inadequate or defective. This can lead to self-doubt and distorted self-image.

3. "If you really loved me, you would..."

Trigger: Manipulates the victim into doing what the manipulator wants.

Intended Effect: Makes the victim feel guilty for not complying and question their commitment to the relationship. This can lead to a loss of personal boundaries and autonomy.

4. "You're being dramatic";

Trigger: Dismisses the victim's feelings and reactions as exaggerated.

Intended Effect: Invalidates the victim's feelings and makes them feel that their concerns are not legitimate. This can lead to self-doubt and emotional repression.

D) Phrases designed to make the victim feel needy, helpless, or that there's something wrong with them - These phrases are designed to make the victim feel emotionally or mentally unstable, needy, or helpless:

1. "You need help" or "You should see a therapist."

Triggers: Implies that the victim is mentally or emotionally unstable.

Intended Effect: Makes the victim feel that there's something wrong with them and question their mental well-being. This can lead to self-doubt and a distorted sense of self.

2. "You're too needy" or "You're too clingy";

Triggers: Makes the victim feel bad about having needs and wanting closeness.

Intended Effect: Makes the victim feel insecure, unwanted, and guilty for expressing their needs. This can lead to self-neglect and fear of abandonment.

3. "I'm just trying to help you";

Trigger: Manipulates the victim into believing that the manipulator has good intentions.

Intended Effect: Causes the victim to doubt their own judgment and ignore the manipulator's harmful behavior. This can lead to a loss of trust in one's own instincts and continued tolerance of the abuse.

4. "You always do this";

Trigger: Generalizing and dismissing the victim's behavior or feelings.

Intended Effect: Makes the victim feel that their actions or feelings are predictable, invalid, or unimportant. This can lead to self-doubt and a loss of confidence in one's own experiences.

Chapter 11: A Tale of Two Mental Illnesses

Victims of narcissism can often be labeled as introverts, just as narcissists can be perceived as extroverts, when the truth is that the narcissist is putting on a facade while the victim of narcissism is dealing with his or her feelings of inadequacy and lack of self-worth. The victim lacks confidence, while the narcissist pretends to be confident in order to exaggerate qualities he does not possess.

This is why the word "empath" is not as positive as it might seem at first glance, because the empath is not necessarily an altruistic individual, but simply someone who empathizes with the suffering of others. This is because they can see themselves through the emotions of others.

The reason many empaths fall victim to narcissistic abuse for the rest of their lives is because the narcissist knows how to pretend to be a victim of their own actions and the consequences of their mistakes in order to gain the empath's empathy.

Narcissists specifically target empaths and choose them for a relationship, seducing them with the clear intention of gaining their trust because narcissists know that empaths are more tolerant of abuse than anyone else. The narcissist's facade of being a victim of the life he has created for himself is not only a demonstration of a lack of responsibility, but also a strategy to gain the empath's sympathy.

The empath, on the other hand, does not fall in love with the narcissist's qualities because they are not there, but instead empathizes with the weakness that the narcissist presents in the form of an illusion. Thus, while the narcissist projects an illusion to make the empath fall in love, the empath, instead of falling in love with a lie, actually falls in love with the projected illusion that represents himself.

The narcissist projects a personality he does not have, and the empath falls in love with the qualities he cannot see in himself, precisely because he has no self-love. It's a match made in hell, because both are mentally ill, albeit manifesting the illness in seemingly contradictory ways. It's as if the empath says, "I don't deserve to be loved, but I can love someone else," while the narcissist says, "I can't love anyone, but I deserve to be loved. Both also apply the same mindset when it comes to a relationship, because they have supplemented their dysfunction in similar ways over the years.

One of the most common mistakes I see empaths make is to assume that they are victims of narcissism rather than victims of their own choices and beliefs. They can't see that they are also mentally ill and instead use narcissism as a trophy of their own superiority over other people, basically acting like a narcissist when they say they love more than other people and have been hurt because of their empathy for others.

This is not healing from narcissistic abuse, it is rationalizing their experience and assimilating it in their mind as a permanent wound. It is like wrapping a box full of garbage in a nice colorful wrapping instead of throwing it outside.

Empaths can only heal from narcissistic abuse if they stop being empathetic to those who are evil. This means developing emotional discernment, because it is the lack of emotional discernment that makes them empathetic to those who can hurt them. It has to be seen as a psychological handicap rather than a cognitive advantage, which it isn't.

I spent many years studying narcissistic abuse, but I couldn't heal until I learned self-love. It takes years of being alone with yourself and finding a reason to live when there is none outside of yourself. You know you can love yourself when you are able to let go of people who don't respect you. Until then, you can't say that love is blind to lack of respect, or that you tolerate the abuse of others because you have more empathy than the average person. That's not love, that's mental illness. When two mentally ill people get together, you get what is called a toxic relationship.

Only when you are able to let go of a disrespectful partner to find peaceful solitude can you understand self-love and only then can you find true love. But here is another challenge: because empaths have been abused in their childhood, they are not likely to understand true love and therefore develop feelings for the right person, just as a narcissist will not see it.

The difference is that while narcissists never find true love because they seek admiration, empaths can find true love as soon as they prioritize respect, and they will learn this as soon as they develop self-love.

Chapter 12: Confusing Self-Love and Narcissism

It sounds like a contradiction to say that empaths need self-love, because it is as if empaths need to become like narcissists, just as narcissists need to look outside themselves for love. However, society denies the empath's self-love when it confuses it with selfishness and egotism, and condemns it as an act of narcissism. But society doesn't know the difference between the two, and can't even tell a narcissist from an empath.

If the average person can't tell the difference between a narcissist and an empath, why should we expect them to tell the difference between selfishness and self-esteem or self-love? They can't! The opinions of the ignorant masses are worthless and can often add to the psychological damage caused by the narcissist. This is especially true if you share the actions of the narcissists in your life with other family members, especially other narcissists.

It is also worth noting that most of the people I have met who claim to be victims of narcissists are narcissists themselves.

Although it is not uncommon for narcissists to label empaths as narcissists, especially to belittle and invalidate them in public, it is also true that narcissists often fall in love with, or at least feel a strong attraction and emotional connection to, other narcissists. This is perhaps the most obvious example of how a narcissist self-destructs as they seek admiration from those who can deceive them in the same way they have deceived others.

For this reason, while the empath has a better chance of recovering from his or her mental illness, the narcissist is more likely to end up heartbroken and lonely later in life, especially in the case of female narcissists.

In the end, the empath can choose to struggle with loneliness and walk through the darkness on the way to rebuilding himself and his life, or he can simply give up and let the narcissist win the game of putting others down by turning the putting down on himself and accepting the lie that he is unworthy of love and success. But the narcissist will never be able to find real love or fulfillment because of his obsession with manipulation and his need to be admired.

The narcissist may even reach a very high level academically and professionally, which makes him work even harder to hide his incompetence and the lies he had to produce to get there. He will also have to live with the constant tension of pretending to be someone he is not to the people he despises but who are attracted to his life precisely because he has been able to manipulate them.

Eventually, the mask falls and everyone sees the narcissist for who he is. But this mask falls more quickly than with other people when the narcissist and the empath meet in a relationship. The empath exhausts himself trying to make the narcissist happy, while the narcissist can never be happy, so he exhausts himself competing to put the empath down. The more love the empath offers, the more hate the narcissist responds with, and in the end the empath simply becomes apathetic.

The narcissist always wins by exhausting others, and they do this by constantly plotting and conspiring for their downfall. But this is also what makes the narcissist regret his behavior later on, because of course he will never meet such an empath in his life. All the narcissists I met would eventually regret losing me and would send me messages to get me to respond to them.

I never responded for the obvious reason that narcissists never change. Their regret is always about themselves and the fact that they lost their favorite toy and the attention it gave them. In the eyes of the narcissist, you are not a real person but an object whose value is the attention you give or the validation they get from others through you or by having you.

The narcissist only regrets his own misfortune in not finding a better toy to manipulate for affection and attention, even though the victim would simply be worse off than before if he got the same person back. This is because the narcissist despises the victim as much as he despises himself. A victim who returns to the abuse is even more degrading in the eyes of the narcissist than one who had to be lied to and manipulated in order to be abused. Thus, the narcissist feels more justified in abusing those who return to him than those who get away.

Chapter 13: The Paradox of Narcissistic Love

The relationship between narcissists and those who see through their veneer presents a perplexing paradox. Counterintuitively, narcissists often show greater respect for people who recognize their true nature, even as they attempt to punish or control them. This stems from the narcissist's distorted view of love, for they equate recognition and confrontation with genuine affection, no matter how dysfunctional that dynamic may be.

This distorted view of love extends to the narcissist's perception of violence. Many narcissists interpret aggressive or abusive behavior as passionate displays of love. This mindset often leads to a karmic cycle in which narcissists are drawn to equally volatile partners who despise them, yet remain trapped in tumultuous relationships that can last for decades. The roles can often be interchangeable as both individuals learn to shift between aggressor, savior, and victim:

- When person A shifts to the role of victim, person B shifts to the role of savior.

- When person B shifts to the role of savior, person A shifts to the role of aggressor.

- When person A becomes the aggressor, person B shifts from being the rescuer to being the victim.

- When person A realizes that he has succeeded in making person B feel helpless, he can switch to the role of rescuer.

- If person B takes advantage of the narcissist's savior transformation and uses revenge, person B becomes the aggressor and person A shifts to the victim state.

Let us examine how valence shifting might apply to the above examples:

1. Aggressor to Victim: A narcissist may shift from being the aggressor to playing the victim in order to manipulate the other person into the role of savior.

For example:

Aggressor: "You're crazy" (questioning reality and perception).

Victim: "I can't believe you're being so mean to me. I'm just trying my best" (Shifting to the victim role to elicit sympathy or make the other person feel guilty).

2. Victim to Aggressor: A narcissist playing the victim may suddenly switch to the aggressor role when he feels he has gained enough sympathy or wants to regain control.

For example:

Victim: "No one else would put up with you" (making the victim feel bad).

Aggressor: "You're so ungrateful after all I've done for you!" (Shifting to the role of aggressor to make the other person feel guilty and indebted).

3. Savior of the aggressor/victim: A narcissist in the role of savior may shift to either aggressor or victim when he doesn't get the admiration or compliance he expects.

For example:

Savior: "I'm just trying to help you" (pretending to have good intentions).

Aggressor: "But you don't listen to me! You're so stubborn!" (Shifting to the aggressor role when her "help" is not accepted).

Victim: "I go out of my way to help you, and this is the thanks I get?" (Shifting to the victim role to elicit guilt or sympathy).

In the dynamic between two narcissists, these valence shifts can occur frequently and rapidly as each person tries to gain the upper hand or maintain control. The roles are interchangeable, and the manipulative tactics used can shift rapidly depending on the situation and the desired outcome.

This triangulation always occurs between a narcissist and whomever they attract into their lives, which may or may not be another narcissist. However, once a person is caught in this cycle, it never ends. The narcissist always plays the victim when the victim develops self-respect and leaves the relationship, and immediately becomes the aggressor when the victim falls into the trap, starting the same cycle of madness all over again.

Empaths fall into the narcissist's traps because the narcissist presents a fictitious or pseudo-realistic condition in which they need to be rescued from a situation that the narcissist has deliberately created or from which they are suffering as a result of their own actions. This is also the typical way in which narcissists are drawn into a relationship with another narcissist.

On the other hand, because these mind games often occur in relationships with narcissists, it is also through such games that a once normal and healthy person can, over time, become a victim of narcissistic abuse and later become a narcissist themselves.

Chapter 14: When Victims Mirror Their Abusers

The phenomenon of victims of narcissistic abuse taking on narcissistic traits themselves is a complex and fascinating aspect of the cycle of abuse. This role reversal, often referred to as reactive narcissism, can manifest in a variety of ways. Here are some examples of how victims can act against narcissists by adopting narcissistic behaviors themselves:

1. The silent treatment: A victim who has endured a long period of being ignored or given the silent treatment by a narcissist may begin to use this tactic themselves. They may become emotionally withdrawn and refuse to communicate with the narcissist as a form of revenge or self-protection.

2. Gaslighting: After experiencing gaslighting from a narcissist, some victims may begin to question and manipulate the narcissist's reality. They may deny events or conversations in an attempt to make the narcissist doubt their own perceptions.

3. Triangulation: Victims may learn to triangulate, bringing other people into their conflicts with the narcissist to gain support or validation, just as the narcissist may have done to them.

4. Grandiosity and self-importance: Some victims may develop an inflated sense of self-importance as a defense mechanism. They may begin to brag about their accomplishments or exaggerate their abilities, mirroring the narcissist's behavior.

5. Lack of empathy: After being exposed to a narcissist's lack of empathy, some victims may become emotionally numb and have difficulty empathizing with others, including the narcissist.

6. Manipulation: Victims may adopt manipulative tactics they've observed in the narcissist, using guilt, shame, or fear to control the narcissist's behavior.

7. Attention seeking: Some victims may begin to crave attention and validation from others, much like the narcissist, in order to rebuild their damaged self-esteem.

8. Revenge seeking: In extreme cases, victims may plot elaborate revenge schemes and focus obsessively on getting back at the narcissist, mirroring the narcissist's tendency to hold grudges and seek revenge.

9. Emotional Withholding: Just as narcissists often withhold affection and approval, some victims may learn to do the same, using emotional withholding as a form of control or punishment.

10. Excessive Criticism: After being constantly criticized by a narcissist, some victims may become hypercritical themselves, constantly finding fault with the narcissist or others.

11. Boundary Violations: After having their boundaries repeatedly violated, some victims may begin to disregard the boundaries of others, including the narcissist, in an attempt to regain control.

12. Projection: Victims may begin to project their own feelings or insecurities onto the narcissist, blaming them for the very things they are feeling or doing.

13. Entitlement: Some victims may develop a sense of entitlement, feeling that they deserve special treatment or exemptions from rules after being subjected to the narcissist's sense of entitlement.

14. Exploitation: Victims may begin to exploit others, including the narcissist, for their own gain, mirroring the exploitative behavior they have experienced.

15. Envy and jealousy: After being the target of a narcissist's envy and jealousy, some victims may become envious and jealous themselves, constantly comparing their lives to others.

16. Arrogance: Victims may adopt an arrogant attitude as a defense mechanism to protect themselves from further emotional harm.

17. Blame shifting: Some victims may begin to blame others, including the narcissist, for their actions in order to avoid taking responsibility for their own behavior.

18. Hypersensitivity to Criticism: Victims may become extremely sensitive to any form of criticism, perceiving it as a personal attack, much as a narcissist would.

19. Need for Adulation: After being deprived of admiration and validation, some victims may develop an excessive need for admiration from others to boost their self-esteem.

20. Disregard for the feelings of others: Victims may begin to disregard the feelings and needs of others, including the narcissist, in order to protect themselves from further emotional pain.

Chapter 15: Power Dynamics in Narcissistic Relationships

There are many real-life stories that illustrate the valence shift in relationships with narcissists and the potential transformation of victims into narcissists themselves. Here are a few common examples:

1. The Gaslighting Spouse:

Maria and John were married for five years. Maria was a narcissist who frequently gaslighted John. She would accuse him of flirting with other women whenever they went out, even though he was faithful. One day, John discovered that Maria was having an affair. When confronted, Maria turned the tables on John, accusing him of being the one who was unfaithful and gaslighting him about her own infidelity.

Valence shift: Exhausted and confused by the constant accusations and now the betrayal, John snapped. He began to mimic Maria's behavior, accusing her of more infidelities and twisting her words. He also decided to "get even" and began flirting with other women, eventually having an affair of his own.

The result: Maria was initially stunned by John's sudden aggression and infidelity, but quickly regained her composure. She played the victim and accused John of being cruel and unloving. John, in turn, used Maria's infidelity to justify his own actions. Their relationship became a constant power struggle in which both parties engaged in a cycle of infidelity, manipulation, and control. John's transformation into a narcissist was complete. He no longer cared about Maria's feelings or the health of their relationship. All he cared about was winning and maintaining control. Their mutual infidelities became ammunition in their ongoing war, with each blaming the other for the demise of their relationship.

2. The Shattered Dream:

Paul and Richard were childhood friends who started a coffee shop together. Paul, with his charisma and vision, took the lead on operations, while Richard, more reserved and meticulous, handled the finances. Unbeknownst to Richard, Paul had narcissistic tendencies that began to surface as the business grew. Whenever something went wrong, Paul would blame Richard for not pulling his weight or not being competent enough. Richard, eager to preserve their friendship and the business, would accept the blame and work harder to make amends.

Valence shift: After a disastrous attempt to expand the cafe, they suffered a significant financial loss. Paul blamed Richard for not securing enough financing and for being too cautious with their marketing strategy. This time, however, Richard didn't back down. He had been quietly compensating for Paul's reckless spending and impulsive decisions, and he had reached his breaking point. Richard retaliated by shifting the blame back onto Paul. He confronted Paul with evidence of his mismanagement, including unauthorized purchases, neglected bills, and ignoring employee concerns. Richard accused Paul of jeopardizing the company and their friendship with his irresponsible behavior. This sudden assertiveness caught Paul off guard and marked a significant shift in their dynamic.

The result: Paul, unable to take responsibility, assumed the role of victim. He accused Richard of being disloyal and unsupportive and claimed that Richard was trying to sabotage him. Their relationship deteriorated as they engaged in a cycle of blame and manipulation. Richard, in his newfound determination to hold Paul accountable, began to develop assertive traits that bordered on aggression. The atmosphere in the café became toxic. Employees were caught in the middle, and the quality of service declined. Customers began to notice the tension, and business slowed. Richard, realizing that their partnership was beyond repair, went to their mutual investors. He presented evidence of Paul's misdeeds, and the investors sided with Richard and demanded that Paul resign. Paul left the business, but the cafe never recovered. The financial losses were too great, and the once-thriving business folded a few months later. The valence shift in Richard's behavior, from passive and accommodating to assertive and confrontational, ultimately led to the end of their friendship and the demise of their shared dream.

3. The Revenge of the Mirror:

Laura and Steve were in a romantic relationship in which Laura was the narcissist. At first, Laura love-bombed Steve, showering him with affection and making him feel like the center of her world. However, once Steve became emotionally involved, Laura began to devalue him, criticizing his appearance, his intelligence, and even his friends.

Valence shift: After months of enduring Laura's criticism and manipulation, Steve suddenly had a change of perspective. He decided that if he couldn't change her, he would join her. He began mimicking her behavior, criticizing her looks and intelligence, and manipulating her emotions. He learned to play the victim when it suited him and turned every argument around on her.

The result: At first, Laura was hurt and shocked by Steve's behavior, but she soon found herself in a constant power struggle. Their relationship became a never-ending battle of criticism and manipulation. Steve took on more and more narcissistic traits, learning to feed off the drama and control. He began to gaslight Laura, causing her to question her own reality and sanity. However, as Steve's narcissism grew, he began to realize that he didn't need Laura anymore. He had learned to feed his newfound narcissistic supply from others-friends, co-workers, even strangers. He began to pull away from Laura, giving her a taste of her own medicine. He would disappear for days, ignoring her calls and messages, only to reappear with cold indifference. Laura, unable to cope with the role reversal, became increasingly desperate and erratic. She tried to win him back, to regain control, but Steve was always one step ahead, manipulating her as she had once manipulated him. Eventually, Steve disappeared from her life completely, leaving Laura a shell of her former self.

4. The Triangulating Mother-in-Law:

Barbara was a narcissist who often interfered with her son Tom's marriage to Lisa. She frequently criticized and complained about Lisa to Tom, playing the victim and claiming that Lisa was not good enough for him. Initially, Lisa would try to reason with Barbara and defend herself, while Tom would try to mediate.

Valence shift: Over time, Barbara's constant manipulation and criticism took a toll on Lisa. She began to adopt narcissistic traits as a defense mechanism against Barbara's abuse. Lisa began to belittle and criticize Tom for not standing up to his mother, mimicking Barbara's critical behavior; play the victim, claiming that both Tom and Barbara were against her and that she was the only one trying to save their marriage; manipulate situations to appear superior to Barbara, such as exaggerating her accomplishments and minimizing Barbara's contributions; demand special treatment from Tom, insisting that he put her needs and desires above all else to make up for his mother's mistreatment of her.

The result: As Lisa took on more narcissistic traits, their marriage became increasingly toxic. Tom felt caught in the middle of a power struggle between his mother and his wife. The constant manipulation and criticism from both sides eventually led Tom to feel overwhelmed and unable to continue the relationship. He filed for divorce, citing the toxic dynamic and irreconcilable differences. Barbara, playing the victim as usual, blamed Lisa for the divorce. Lisa, in turn, blamed Tom and Barbara for the failure of their marriage, refusing to acknowledge her own role in the dynamic.

Chapter 16: The Insidious Nature of Narcissistic Abuse

At first glance, the idea that victims of narcissistic abuse may themselves exhibit narcissistic traits may seem counterintuitive or even paradoxical, but as we delve deeper into the psychological mechanisms at play, we begin to see how this response can emerge as a coping strategy in the face of prolonged trauma and manipulation.

However, such behaviors in victims are fundamentally different from those of true narcissists, both in their origin and in their potential for change. Määttä et al. (2012) explain that victims can sometimes adopt similar behaviors as a coping mechanism. It is a form of psychological survival, a way for the victim to navigate the treacherous waters of their abusive relationship. Unlike true narcissists, victims who exhibit these behaviors usually retain the capacity for self-reflection and may feel remorse for their actions. These behaviors in victims are typically a learned response to trauma rather than an ingrained personality trait.

The concept of "trauma enforced bonding" or "trauma enforced attachment," as described by Raghavan and Doychak (2015), provides a framework for understanding this complex dynamic. In the face of ongoing abuse and manipulation, victims may begin to lose their sense of self and gradually adopt aspects of their abuser's worldview or behaviors. This process can be seen as a way for victims to make sense of their experiences and maintain some semblance of control in an otherwise chaotic and unpredictable environment.

Howard (2022) further elucidates this phenomenon, describing it as a form of "living martyrdom. In this state, victims may temporarily take on some of their abuser's characteristics as a way of coping with and understanding their traumatic experiences. This mimicry can serve several purposes: it can help the victim predict and control their abuser's behavior, provide a sense of empowerment in an otherwise powerless situation, or even serve as a misguided attempt to connect with the abuser on their own terms. However, victims who engage in these behaviors may experience guilt or remorse for their actions, creating an internal conflict that serves as additional distress as they struggle to reconcile with their core values and sense of self.

Lahav et al. (2020) provide further insight into the complex emotional landscape of abuse victims, noting that they often struggle with both internal and external aggression as they process their trauma. This internal struggle is markedly different from the lack of empathy and self-reflection seen in true narcissistic personality disorder. The presence of this internal conflict can actually be seen as a positive sign, indicating that the victim has not completely lost touch with his or her authentic self and values.

The ability of victims to recover from narcissistic abuse and shed these adopted behaviors is influenced by several factors, including the duration and intensity of the abuse, the victim's personal resilience, and access to appropriate support and resources. Ghodratollahifard et al. (2020) highlight the particular vulnerability of those who have experienced childhood trauma, finding that early abuse, combined with maladaptive emotional regulation strategies, is associated with a higher risk of developing personality disorder symptoms later in life. This underscores the critical importance of early intervention and support for victims of narcissistic abuse, particularly children and adolescents who may be at increased risk for long-term psychological sequelae.

Nevertheless, recovery is possible even for those who have experienced prolonged or severe abuse. Maffini et al. (2021) highlight the effectiveness of trauma-focused cognitive-behavioral therapy in helping victims of abuse process their experiences and develop healthier coping mechanisms. This type of therapy can be particularly beneficial in addressing the maladaptive behaviors that may have developed as a result of the abuse, helping victims reconnect with their authentic selves and rebuild a sense of agency and self-worth. The path to recovery often involves a multifaceted approach that addresses both the psychological and practical aspects of healing. This may include individual therapy, support groups, education about narcissistic abuse and its effects, and practical assistance in areas such as housing, employment, and legal support. The goal is not only to help victims process their trauma, but also to empower them to rebuild their lives and reclaim their sense of self.

The recovery process is rarely linear and may include setbacks and challenges along the way. Victims may struggle with trust issues, hypervigilance, and difficulty forming healthy relationships even after leaving the abusive situation. These ongoing challenges underscore the need for long-term support and understanding from both professionals and the victim's personal support network.

Left unaddressed, a victim of narcissistic abuse may be at risk for developing more enduring narcissistic traits themselves, potentially perpetuating the cycle of abuse in their future relationships. This potential for intergenerational transmission of abuse underscores the critical importance of breaking the cycle through education, awareness, and accessible mental health support. By recognizing the signs of narcissistic abuse and providing timely intervention, we can help prevent the perpetuation of these harmful patterns and support victims on their journey to healing and recovery.

Chapter 17: The Double-Edged Sword of Narcissistic Abuse

In the complicated landscape of relationships involving narcissists, the dynamics can shift dramatically, often leading to intense emotional confrontations and, in some cases, extreme actions by those who were once victims. These shifts can manifest in a variety of ways, including victims resorting to violence or abandoning their abusers in dire circumstances. The following real-life stories and cases illustrate the profound effects of narcissistic abuse and the lengths to which victims may go to escape or retaliate.

The Menendez Brothers Case (1989): Lyle and Erik Menendez were convicted of murdering their parents, Jose and Kitty Menendez, in their Beverly Hills mansion. The brothers claimed that they had suffered years of sexual, emotional, and physical abuse at the hands of their narcissistic and abusive father. The brothers were ultimately sentenced to life in prison without the possibility of parole.

The Betty Broderick Case (1989): After enduring years of emotional abuse and gaslighting at the hands of her narcissistic husband, Dan Broderick, Betty Broderick shot and killed Dan and his new wife, Linda. Betty had become increasingly unstable after Dan left her for his younger assistant, Linda, and used his legal expertise to manipulate the divorce proceedings.

The story of Ruchika Girhotra (1990): Ruchika Girhotra was a 14-year-old girl who was sexually abused by S.P.S. Rathore, a senior police officer in Haryana, India. Rathore exhibited narcissistic tendencies and used his power to intimidate and abuse Ruchika. Despite the harassment, Ruchika and her family fought back and filed a complaint against Rathore. Tragically, Ruchika committed suicide three years later due to the ongoing harassment and social stigma. Her family continued the legal battle, and in 2009, Rathore was finally convicted.

The Clara Harris case (2002): Clara Harris was a Texas dentist who discovered that her husband, David Harris, was having an affair with his receptionist. David exhibited narcissistic traits and had a history of infidelity. In a fit of rage, Clara drove her car over David several times in a hotel parking lot, killing him. Clara was later convicted of murder and sentenced to 20 years in prison.

The case of Mary Winkler (2006): Mary Winkler was a Tennessee woman who shot and killed her husband, Matthew Winkler, a minister with a history of narcissistic and abusive behavior. Mary endured years of emotional and physical abuse before taking extreme action. She was later convicted of voluntary manslaughter and sentenced to three years in prison.

John Edwards and Rielle Hunter affair (2006): John Edwards, a former U.S. senator, was involved in a highly publicized extramarital affair with Rielle Hunter while his wife, Elizabeth Edwards, was battling cancer. John, who exhibited narcissistic tendencies, sought validation and admiration outside of his marriage. Rielle, initially a victim of John's manipulation, eventually used the affair to gain financial and social leverage. The affair led to the dissolution of John's political career and left him struggling with public humiliation and personal loss.

The case of Jodi Arias and Travis Alexander (2008): The relationship between Jodi Arias and Travis Alexander was tumultuous and marked by emotional manipulation and control. Travis, who exhibited narcissistic traits, often belittled and manipulated Jodi. Over time, Jodi's behavior became increasingly erratic and obsessive. In 2008, the relationship culminated in a violent confrontation in which Jodi murdered Travis at his home in Mesa, Arizona.

The Gypsy Rose Blanchard Case (2015): Gypsy Rose Blanchard was a longtime victim of her mother, Dee Dee Blanchard, who exhibited narcissistic and abusive behavior, fabricated illnesses for Gypsy, and subjected her to unnecessary medical procedures. To escape her mother's abuse, Gypsy conspired with her then-boyfriend to murder Dee Dee. Gypsy manipulated her boyfriend into committing the crime, mirroring the manipulative tactics she learned from her mother.

The Sally Challen case (2019): Sally Challen was convicted of murdering her husband, Richard Challen, in 2010 after enduring decades of psychological abuse. Richard exhibited narcissistic traits and subjected Sally to coercive control. In 2019, Sally's conviction was overturned and she was released from prison after a successful appeal that recognized the impact of coercive control and domestic violence.

Chapter 18: The Enduring Allure of Toxic Bonds

The longevity of toxic bonds with narcissists is often sustained by the victim's internalized sense of hopelessness and the narcissist's skillful psychological manipulation. But the effects of such dysfunctional relationships ripple outward, affecting entire families. Children raised in homes dominated by narcissistic abuse witness constant conflict and come to normalize violence as an inherent part of intimate relationships. Their mentally ill caregivers reinforce this distorted worldview, insisting that the chaos and aggression they experience is perfectly normal.

As a result, these children often grow into adults who find peace unsettling and unconsciously create drama to recreate the familiar turmoil of their upbringing. Some even come to equate conflict and reconciliation with true love, unable to imagine a healthy, stable partnership. As some mentally disturbed women have told me: "If we don't fight and make up, how will I know you love me? And how will I know if you really love me, or if you might otherwise leave me?"

The dynamics created by narcissists are extremely compelling because they are characterized by intense emotional experiences and psychological manipulation. This is why they are so often portrayed in various forms of media, including literature and film, where such relationships are often romanticized. They often follow a pattern in which one person, typically exhibiting narcissistic traits, exerts control and influence over their partner, who becomes emotionally dependent on the narcissist.

The widespread fascination with these relationships can be seen in the popularity of novels such as E.L. James' "Fifty Shades of Grey," which has become a cultural phenomenon. The book and its sequels explore the complex dynamics between the protagonists, Christian Grey and Anastasia Steele, whose relationship is marked by power plays and elements of control often associated with narcissistic relationships. In addition, the character of Christian Grey in Fifty Shades of Grey can be seen as a modern counterpart to the Byronic hero, a character type that is both appealing and repulsive due to his complex, often dark personality. This archetype, seen in characters such as Mr. Rochester from Charlotte Brontë's Jane Eyre, embodies qualities of arrogance, a troubled past, and a propensity for emotional manipulation, traits often associated with narcissistic personality disorder.

Fantasy literature also provides compelling examples of these dynamics, particularly in novels that feature vampires. In Anne Rice's "Interview with the Vampire," the relationship between Louis de Pointe du Lac and his creator, Lestat de Lioncourt, is one of emotional dependency and manipulation. Lestat, a charismatic and narcissistic figure, exerts control over Louis, who struggles with his new existence and the moral implications of being a vampire. The sequel, "The Vampire Lestat," delves deeper into Lestat's backstory, revealing the complex power dynamics and emotional manipulation that characterize his relationships with other vampires.

By equating emotional abuse with love and relationship dynamics, these fictional stories also contribute to the normalization of psychological abuse, especially narcissistic manipulation. People have become accustomed to accepting mental illness as a part of life, and then wonder why their relationships are such unfulfilling misery when they show signs of toxicity, and why a large percentage of the world's women are unmarried and unable to find a husband.

According to recent projections by Morgan Stanley, 45 percent of women between the ages of 25 and 44 in the United States will be single by 2030. This is the highest percentage of single women in this age group in recorded history. Similar trends are emerging globally, with the proportion of single women in China expected to rise from 39 percent in 2021 to about 44 percent in 2030. If these patterns continue, about half or more of women in major economies such as the United States and China could be single and childless by 2040, with similar percentages likely in other parts of the world.

Meanwhile, about 20 percent of the world's population is estimated to have narcissistic traits, and this percentage is growing, meaning that more and more people will need to understand how to evaluate potential relationships and overcome narcissistic abuse in a variety of contexts. Several factors contribute to the rapid spread of narcissistic traits in today's society:

1. Social media and technology: The rise of platforms that encourage self-promotion and curated self-presentation has normalized excessive self-absorption and preoccupation with appearance. Studies have linked problematic smartphone use to increased narcissistic tendencies.

2. Societal emphasis on self-esteem: Well-intentioned efforts to promote self-esteem, especially in educational settings, may have inadvertently promoted narcissistic tendencies by focusing on self-esteem without emphasizing empathy and social responsibility.

3. Media influence: Increased exposure to celebrity culture and idealized lifestyles through various media channels may reinforce narcissistic aspirations and unrealistic expectations.

4. Economic factors: Some researchers argue that economic systems that reward self-promotion and individualistic achievement may inadvertently reinforce narcissistic behaviors.

5. Decline in community involvement: As traditional community structures weaken, there may be fewer opportunities for individuals to develop empathy and social awareness through collective experiences.

Chapter 19: Narcissistic Friendships

The normalization of narcissistic traits, the excitement that pervades romantic novels and movies that depict narcissistic behavior, and the general admiration for celebrities who exhibit narcissistic attitudes leads society to become unconsciously attracted to such personalities and even tolerant of the abuse they receive. This popularity of narcissism becomes even more appealing to the narcissists themselves, who look up to each other as role models.

Consequently, just as narcissists develop an appreciation for other narcissists because of their nature to admire narcissistic traits in others, and end up in relationships with other narcissists where they receive the karmic payback for what they do to others, they also seem to find comfort in friends who exhibit narcissistic traits. These are the people who validate them and encourage their narcissistic behavior. Such people never tell them to improve or change and instead praise their abuse and disrespect of others.

Narcissists love this because they have the brain of a child. They love to be favored and praised for acting like an immature child.

On the other hand, only the morons see the narcissist as someone worthy of admiration, and not surprisingly, many of these morons are narcissists themselves. It is like watching a legion of demons gather, with one demon being more devious and manipulative than the others who look up to him for comfort and affirmation.

For these reasons, I believe that what attracts the narcissist to the empath is the same reason he hates the empath, and that is the empath's naivety. This is expressed in a simple question that many narcissists ask the victim: Why do you want to be with me?

Such women cannot understand why someone would know they are evil and still want to be with them and make them feel validated.

The concept of the bad boy represents the other side of this phenomenon, because women with a negative character are attracted to men of the same nature. The worse a woman is, the more she is attracted to men of similar character. That is why they all end up alone after 40 and still think that the problem is not with them but with the men they meet, as if they were not precisely describing narcissistic men and not the entire male population.

Those who know someone is evil will treat them as such, which makes it easy for the evil personality to stop pretending, relax, and feel accepted. They confuse this with love, except there's no love in these relationships, just narcissists mirroring each other. This is why they end up falling in love with the men who hurt them.

These women expect the narcissistic men to return their love because they are the only type of man they can be truly attracted to, and when they say, "I left him because he was a narcissist," they are hiding what they later confirm to be the truth: they were abandoned by a narcissist.

To the narcissist, there are only two types of people - the strong and the weak. The strong are those who take advantage of others, while the weak are those who need others to survive. So they use the weak, but they are attracted to the strong, which means they are attracted to the attention that an empath provides, just as they are attracted to the validation that a narcissist provides. They love the strong with their abuse as much as they fear it.

Here are the stories of people who complain about spouses but keep going back to them. Trapped in their own delusions, narcissists act as if the only way to survive is to ally themselves with those they perceive as strong and create smear campaigns around those they perceive as threats to their insecurities.

They are attracted to the attention of the empath as much as they are repelled by his qualities, and they are attracted to the validation of another narcissist as much as they are afraid of being abandoned. Typically, narcissists waver in their relationships with empaths and other narcissists for these reasons.

However, the level of insecurity they feel can be so deep that they will go to great lengths in their smear campaigns to invalidate someone, which means that they are always destroying their own relationships.

Chapter 20: Transactional Relationships

Perhaps the most common paradox of narcissistic behavior is that they seek the attention of those they despise. They do this only as long as such people are useful to them, and later discard and ignore them when that is no longer the case. In the meantime, they will denigrate the reputation of such people and even spread false rumors that contradict the kind of value they see in the other person. Such was the case of a French writer I met in Greece who insinuated to people that I had dead cats in my house, or that cats had been disappearing in the area since I arrived. He was trying to make people believe that I kill cats for fun, playing on their paranoid thoughts, and people were mentally retarded enough to believe him, which is why I had disagreements with some who claimed that I had poisoned their cat.

There are so many stupid people on this planet that they will believe anything you tell them, even the most ridiculous things. They are prone to paranoid personality disorder, which the narcissist takes full advantage of. The narcissist is good enough at deceiving others to get his way, no matter how absurd what he says may be, because he knows people are stupid enough to believe him.

Narcissists also believe that everyone is out to steal what little they have, so they also believe that if they share and teach what they know, they will lose the advantage they have over others. Instead, they try to gain and maintain that advantage by gathering information about other people, either through gossip or through false displays of altruism and friendship. They talk without talking, wanting to gather information but not revealing anything about themselves or what they know. You can see this clearly when they refuse to answer the same questions they ask you.

A narcissist's level of intelligence is limited to themselves, which is why they may appear to be experts at deception, manipulation, and lying, but are incredibly stupid at everything else. They are unable to empathize with others or see things from their perspective. Narcissists do not know how to trust, cooperate, or work with others because they see everything as competition, so they see their interactions as exchanges instead. If there is nothing to exchange, they would rather abandon the other individual or even let them die alone. They do not understand the value of sharing thoughts and insights because it is not part of their reality. In fact, narcissists have nothing but contempt for a partner or friend who is ill and would rather party all night with other people than stay next to a sick spouse.

A perfect analogy for this is the pharmaceutical industry, which profits from people's illness and lets those who can't afford their drugs die, while at the same time forcing doctors to prescribe certain procedures under threat of losing their license if they don't. This is what I call bullying at the highest level, with the protection of the law and governments. Doctors who try to break out of this system by prescribing more effective treatments are thrown in jail.It is exhausting to deal with narcissists because they are constantly sucking the energy out of others and acting as energy vampires in every area, incapable of giving any support or recognition. They are obsessed with taking as much as they can from others, especially through legal means, and it's not surprising that many of them seek connections in government and government institutions. They are obsessed with power because they know that with more power they can abuse more people with fewer consequences.

Narcissists are plagued by a self-centered view of the world that is often filled with stereotypes, discrimination, and prejudice. They are quick to judge people, forming an opinion in the first 5 seconds and then spending the rest of their time trying to prove that their observations are correct. This creates a situation where other people constantly feel devalued and disrespected as they are forced to prove themselves to people who can never truly be convinced.

Narcissists are incapable of changing their minds, incapable of seeing other people's perspectives or learning from their own mistakes, incapable of understanding that their views may be completely wrong or influenced by their limited experience and worldview. Instead, they rely on preconceived notions to navigate the world around them and justify their opinions.

When dealing with narcissists, we often find ourselves trying to prove our worth and convince the narcissist of our value, but this is a futile effort because the narcissist has no interest in listening, learning, or growing from the experience. They are solely focused on their own views and will not change them no matter how much evidence is presented.

This creates a sense of frustration and inadequacy in individuals who are constantly being judged without any real reason or evidence. Over time, dealing with narcissists can have a significant negative impact on an individual's mental health. Dealing with narcissists can contribute significantly to anxiety, depression, and other mental health problems. This is especially true when dealing with narcissists on a regular basis, as the drain becomes more intense and harder to escape, especially in an office environment. This creates a sense of disconnection that can be difficult to overcome.

After a period of being around narcissists, exhausted, we may fall into apathy and lose motivation for the things that once brought us joy, and that is exactly what they want - the destruction of the lives of those who threaten their existence. They try to exhaust the lights of the world by demeaning them and making them apathetic. They are killers of joy. They are what we call toxic personalities. We call them toxic because they poison us - they dull our senses, steal our vitality, exhaust us physically and mentally, and make us act irrationally.

Chapter 21: Understanding and Treating Narcissism

Recent advances in brain imaging and cognitive research have shed new light on narcissistic personality disorder (NPD), offering new insights into why people with this condition behave the way they do. This growing understanding not only helps explain narcissistic traits, but also points to more effective treatments.

At the heart of NPD lies a series of differences in brain function, particularly in areas responsible for self-awareness, empathy, and emotional control. The prefrontal cortex, a region critical to these functions, shows reduced activity in people with NPD. This helps explain their difficulty with impulse control, lack of empathy, and struggles with managing emotions. But the story doesn't end there. The brain is a complex network, and in NPD, the connections between different areas are also altered.

For example, the connection between the prefrontal cortex and the amygdala, a region involved in processing emotions, is disrupted.

This leads to heightened emotional responses and a tendency to perceive even minor criticism as a major threat.

Another key player is the brain's reward system. In people with NPD, this system is overly sensitive to praise and admiration, but less responsive to negative feedback. This imbalance fuels the constant need for validation and difficulty learning from mistakes that characterize narcissistic behavior.

The mirror neuron system, which helps us understand and empathize with others, also functions differently in NPD. Reduced activity in this system may explain why people with NPD have difficulty connecting emotionally with others and often treat people as objects rather than as individuals with their own feelings and needs.

In addition, the default mode network, a set of brain regions that are active when we're thinking about ourselves or others, shows altered patterns in NPD. This may contribute to the narcissist's tendency to interpret everything in terms of how it affects them, often neglecting the perspectives of others.

While these brain differences paint a complex picture, it's important to note that the brain can change. This concept, known as neuroplasticity, offers hope for treatment. It suggests that with the right interventions, these neural patterns can be reshaped. But the development of NPD isn't just about brain structure. It's a complex interplay of genetics, childhood experiences, and the environment. Certain genetic variations may increase the risk of developing narcissistic traits, but these genes interact with life experiences, especially during childhood. Experiences of neglect, abuse, or excessive praise can significantly affect brain development and contribute to narcissistic traits.

Recent research has also begun to explore how chronic stress and inflammation may play a role in NPD. Long-term stress can disrupt the body's stress response system, potentially contributing to the emotional instability seen in NPD.

Understanding these biological underpinnings has important implications for treatment. Traditional talk therapies have often had limited success with NPD, possibly because they don't address the underlying brain differences. However, new approaches are emerging that take these neurological factors into account. For example, neurofeedback techniques aim to increase activity in the prefrontal cortex, potentially improving emotional regulation. Some researchers are exploring medications that target specific neurotransmitter systems involved in NPD, although this approach requires careful study to ensure safety and efficacy.

Several psychotherapeutic approaches show promise for the treatment of NPD:

1. Transference-focused psychotherapy (TFP) aims to address the fragmented internal representations of self and others that contribute to narcissistic behavior.

2. Mentalization-based treatment (MBT) focuses on improving the ability to understand one's own and others' mental states, potentially enhancing empathy and social cognition.

3. Schema therapy works to identify and change deep-seated beliefs and patterns that underlie narcissistic traits.

While these therapies differ in their specific approaches, they all aim to reshape the neural pathways associated with self-perception and interpersonal relationships.

The growing understanding of the biological basis of NPD also underscores the importance of early intervention. Identifying at-risk individuals early and providing appropriate support could potentially alter the course of narcissistic personality development.

As research continues, we can expect even more targeted and personalized treatments for NPD. The integration of brain imaging into treatment planning may allow therapies to be tailored to an individual's specific neural patterns. By bridging the gap between neuroscience and psychology, we're moving toward more effective ways to treat this challenging condition. While NPD remains complex, these findings provide a path forward that promises better outcomes for individuals with narcissistic traits and those around them.

Chapter 22: Unmasking the Narcissist

At the heart of narcissistic behavior is a paradoxical mix of grandiosity and insecurity, a constant need for admiration coupled with a profound lack of empathy. This toxic combination creates a destructive force that ripples through families, workplaces, and society at large. As we have seen, narcissists are driven by an insatiable desire for power and control, often resorting to manipulation, gaslighting, and emotional abuse to maintain their perceived superiority.

The constant attacks, both overt and covert, can leave individuals feeling hopeless and questioning their sanity. This psychological warfare is particularly insidious because it often goes unnoticed by others, with the average person denying or dismissing the evidence before their eyes. This societal blindness to narcissistic abuse perpetuates a cycle of victimization and allows narcissists to continue their destructive behavior unchecked.

The effects of narcissistic abuse extend far beyond the immediate victim, affecting entire families and even future generations. Children raised in homes dominated by narcissistic parents often internalize distorted views of love and relationships, equating conflict and reconciliation with genuine affection. This normalization of toxic dynamics can lead to the perpetuation of abusive patterns as victims unconsciously seek out or recreate familiar chaotic environments in their adult relationships. The increasing rates of single and childless individuals in major economies can be attributed, in part, to the challenges of navigating relationships in a world where narcissistic behavior is becoming more commonplace.

Popular culture often romanticizes these intense, emotionally charged relationships, as evidenced by the success of novels featuring narcissists. This cultural fascination with narcissistic dynamics contributes to the normalization of psychological abuse and can make it more difficult for victims to recognize and escape toxic situations.

Constant exposure to their judgmental, self-centered worldview can lead to anxiety, depression, and a pervasive sense of inadequacy in their victims. Narcissists' inability to change their minds or consider alternative perspectives creates an exhausting dynamic in which others are constantly forced to prove their worth, often to no avail. This relentless devaluation can undermine self-esteem and lead to a loss of motivation and joy in life.

Societal recognition of the prevalence and destructive nature of narcissistic behavior is essential to creating a supportive environment for victims and holding perpetrators accountable. By exposing the destructive power behind narcissistic behavior and understanding its far-reaching consequences, we can begin to develop strategies to combat its influence and foster healthier, more empathetic connections in our personal lives and in society as a whole. With increased awareness, support, and a commitment to personal growth, it is possible to break free from the cycle of toxicity and reclaim one's sense of self-worth.

Glossary

Abuse: Harmful or cruel treatment of another person. In the context of NPD, this can include emotional, psychological, or physical mistreatment.

Amygdala: A region of the brain involved in processing emotions. In individuals with NPD, the connection between the amygdala and prefrontal cortex is often disrupted, leading to heightened emotional responses.

Byronic hero: A character archetype often associated with narcissistic traits, characterized by a complex, often dark personality that is both appealing and repulsive.

Cluster B personality disorders: A group of personality disorders characterized by dramatic, overly emotional, or erratic thinking or behavior. NPD is classified within this group.

Covert Hostility: A subtle form of aggression where the narcissist expresses hostility indirectly, often through passive-aggressive behaviors or manipulation.

Default mode network: A set of brain regions active when thinking about oneself or others. In NPD, this network shows altered patterns, contributing to self-centered interpretation of events.

Empath: An individual who is highly sensitive to the emotions and feelings of others. Empaths are often drawn to narcissists, creating a dysfunctional relationship dynamic.

Emotional withholding: A tactic used by narcissists (and sometimes their victims) to control or punish others by withholding affection or approval.

Gaslighting: A form of psychological manipulation in which the narcissist makes the victim question their own perceptions, memories, or sanity.

Grandiosity: An inflated sense of self-importance, a key characteristic of NPD.

Lack of empathy: The inability to understand or share the feelings of others, a hallmark trait of NPD.

Manipulation: The act of controlling or influencing someone in a clever or unscrupulous way. Narcissists often use manipulation to achieve their goals.

Mentalization-based treatment (MBT): A psychotherapeutic approach that focuses on improving the ability to understand one's own and others' mental states, potentially enhancing empathy and social cognition in individuals with NPD.

Mirror neuron system: A network in the brain that helps us understand and empathize with others. This system shows reduced activity in individuals with NPD.

Narcissistic Personality Disorder (NPD): A mental health condition characterized by an inflated sense of self-importance, a deep need for excessive attention and admiration, and a lack of empathy for others.

Neuroplasticity: The brain's ability to form new neural connections and change its structure. This concept offers hope for treating NPD through targeted interventions.

Prefrontal cortex: A region of the brain critical for self-awareness, empathy, and emotional control. Individuals with NPD often show reduced activity in this area.

Reward system: The brain's mechanism for processing pleasure and motivation. In NPD, this system is overly sensitive to praise but less responsive to negative feedback.

Scapegoat: A person who is blamed or criticized for the wrongdoings, mistakes, or faults of others, especially within a family or group dynamic controlled by a narcissist.

Schema therapy: A psychotherapeutic approach that works to identify and change deep-seated beliefs and patterns underlying narcissistic traits.

Self-abasement: The act of humiliating or belittling oneself. Narcissists often use this tactic on their victims to maintain control.

Self-deprecation: The act of belittling or undervaluing oneself, often used as a defense mechanism or to appear humble. Example: "Oh, I'm just a terrible cook. You really shouldn't expect much from my cooking."

Self-love: A state of appreciation for oneself that grows from actions that support physical, psychological, and spiritual growth. In the context of healing from narcissistic abuse, developing self-love is crucial.

Transference-focused psychotherapy (TFP): A psychotherapeutic approach that aims to address the fragmented internal representations of self and others that contribute to narcissistic behavior.

Trauma enforced bonding: A psychological phenomenon where victims of abuse form strong emotional attachments to their abusers, often seen in relationships involving narcissists.

Trigger phrases: Specific words or sentences used by narcissists to elicit particular emotional responses in their victims, often designed to manipulate, gaslight, or dismiss the victim's experiences.

Valence shift: A change in the emotional charge or significance of a situation or relationship. In the context of NPD, this can refer to how victims may adopt narcissistic traits as a coping mechanism.

Victim: An individual who has suffered from narcissistic abuse. Victims may sometimes adopt narcissistic traits themselves as a defense mechanism.

Bibliography

American Psychiatric Association. (2013). Diagnostic and statistical manual of mental disorders (5th ed.).

Arias, J. (2008). The case of Jodi Arias and Travis Alexander: Manipulation and murder.

Blanchard, G. R. (2015). The Gypsy Rose Blanchard case: Abuse and retaliation.

Brontë, C. (1847). Jane Eyre. Smith, Elder & Co.

Broderick, B. (1989). The Betty Broderick case: Emotional abuse and retaliation.

Challen, S. (2019). The Sally Challen case: Coercive control and legal appeal.

Edwards, J. (2006). John Edwards and Rielle Hunter affair: Political scandal and personal loss.

Ghodratollahifard, M., Mohammadkhani, P., Pourshahbaz, A., & Dolatshahi, B. (2020). Childhood trauma and the development of personality disorders. Journal of Child Psychology and Psychiatry, 61(7), 789-796.

Girhotra, R. (1990). The story of Ruchika Girhotra: Abuse and legal battle.

Harris, C. (2002). The Clara Harris case: Infidelity and murder.

Howard, J. (2022). Living martyrdom: Understanding the emotional landscape of abuse victims. Psychology Today.

Lahav, Y., Stein, D., Ginzburg, K., & Solomon, Z. (2020). Internal and external aggression in victims of narcissistic abuse. Journal of Traumatic Stress, 33(2), 155-165.

Maffini, C. S., Goodman, G. S., Lyons, K. E., Newton, E. K., & Ogle, C. M. (2021). Trauma-focused cognitive-behavioral therapy for victims of narcissistic abuse. Clinical Psychology Review, 83, 101935.

Määttä, K., Uusiautti, S., & Määttä, M. (2012). Victims of narcissistic abuse. Journal of Personality Disorders, 26(6), 847-868.

Menendez Brothers Case (1989). Lyle and Erik Menendez convicted of murdering their parents.

Morgan Stanley. (2021). Projections on single women in the United States and China.

Pew Research Center. (2018). Reading habits in the United States.

Rice, A. (1976). Interview with the vampire. Alfred A. Knopf.

Rice, A. (1985). The vampire Lestat. Alfred A. Knopf.

Various authors. Neuroplasticity and treatment approaches for narcissistic personality disorder.

Various authors. Recent advances in brain imaging and cognitive research on narcissistic personality disorder.

Various authors. Transference-focused psychotherapy (TFP), mentalization-based treatment (MBT), and schema therapy for NPD.

World Health Organization (WHO). Global suicide rates.

Book Review Request

Dear reader,

Thank you for purchasing this book! I would love to know your opinion. Writing a book review helps in understanding the readers and also impacts other readers' purchasing decisions. Your opinion matters. Please write a book review!

Your kindness is greatly appreciated!

About the Author

Dan Desmarques is a renowned author with a remarkable track record in the literary world. With an impressive portfolio of 28 Amazon bestsellers, including eight #1 bestsellers, Dan is a respected figure in the industry. Drawing on his background as a college professor of academic and creative writing, as well as his experience as a seasoned business consultant, Dan brings a unique blend of expertise to his work. His profound insights and transformational content appeal to a wide audience, covering topics as diverse as personal growth, success, spirituality, and the deeper meaning of life. Through his writing, Dan empowers readers to break free from limitations, unlock their inner potential, and embark on a journey of self-discovery and transformation. In a competitive self-help market, Dan's exceptional talent and inspiring stories make him a standout author, motivating readers to engage with his books and embark on a path of personal growth and enlightenment.

Also Written by the Author

1. 66 Days to Change Your Life: 12 Steps to Effortlessly Remove Mental Blocks, Reprogram Your Brain and Become a Money Magnet
2. A New Way of Being: How to Rewire Your Brain and Take Control of Your Life
3. Abnormal: How to Train Yourself to Think Differently and Permanently Overcome Evil Thoughts
4. Alignment: The Process of Transmutation Within the Mechanics of Life
5. Audacity: How to Make Fast and Efficient Decisions in Any Situation
6. Christ Cult Codex: The Untold Secrets of the Abrahamic Religions and the Cult of Jesus
7. Codex Illuminatus: Quotes & Sayings of Dan

Desmarques

8. Collective Consciousness: How to Transcend Mass Consciousness and Become One With the Universe
9. Creativity: Everything You Always Wanted to Know About How to Use Your Imagination to Create Original Art That People Admire
10. Deception: When Everything You Know about God is Wrong
11. Demigod: What Happens When You Transcend The Human Nature?
12. Discernment: How Do Your Emotions Affect Moral Decision-Making?
13. Eclipsing Mediocrity: How to Unveil Hidden Realities and Master Life's Challenges
14. Fearless: Powerful Ways to Get Abundance Flowing into Your Life
15. Feel, Think and Grow Rich: 4 Elements to Attract Success in Life
16. Find Your Flow: How to Get Wisdom and Knowledge from God
17. Holistic Psychology: 77 Secrets about the Mind That They Don't Want You to Know

18. How to Change the World: The Path of Global Ascension Through Consciousness

19. How to Get Lucky: How to Change Your Mind and Get Anything in Life

20. How to Improve Your Self-Esteem: 34 Essential Life Lessons Everyone Should Learn to Find Genuine Happiness

21. How to Study and Understand Anything: Discovering The Secrets of the Greatest Geniuses in History

22. Legacy: How to Build a Life Worth Remembering

23. Religious Leadership: The 8 Rules Behind Successful Congregations

24. Reset: How to Observe Life Through the Hidden Dimensions of Reality and Change Your Destiny

25. Resilience: The Art of Confronting Reality Against the Odds

26. Singularity: What to Do When You Lose Hope in Everything

27. Spiritual Warfare: What You Need to Know About Overcoming Adversity

28. Starseed: Secret Teachings about Heaven and the Future of Humanity

29. Technocracy: The New World Order of the Illuminati and The Battle Between Good and Evil

30. The 10 Laws of Transmutation: The Multidimensional Power of Your Subconscious Mind

31. The 14 Karmic Laws of Love: How to Develop a Healthy and Conscious Relationship With Your Soulmate

32. The 33 Laws of Persistence: How to Overcome Obstacles and Upgrade Your Mindset for Success

33. The 36 Laws of Happiness: How to Solve Urgent Problems and Create a Better Future

34. The Alchemy of Truth: Embracing Change and Transcending Time

35. The Antagonists: What Makes a Successful Person Different?

36. The Antichrist: The Grand Plan of Total Global Enslavement

37. The Awakening: How to Turn Darkness Into Light and Ascend to Higher Dimensions of Existence

38. The Egyptian Mysteries: Essential Hermetic Teachings for a Complete Spiritual Reformation

39. The Evil Within: The Spiritual Battle in Your Mind Deception: When Everything You Know about God is

Wrong

40. The Game of Life and How to Play It: How to Get Anything You Want in Life

41. The Hidden Language of God: How to Find a Balance Between Freedom and Responsibility

42. The Most Powerful Quotes: 400 Motivational Quotes and Sayings

43. The Secret Beliefs of The Illuminati: The Complete Truth About Manifesting Money Using The Law of Attraction That is Being Hidden From You

44. The Secret Empire: The Hidden Truth Behind the Power Elite and the Knights of the New World Order

45. The Secret Science of the Soul: How to Transcend Common Sense and Get What You Really Want From Life

46. The Spiritual Laws of Money: The 31 Best-kept Secrets to Life-long Abundance

47. The Spiritual Mechanics of Love: Secrets They Don't Want You to Know about Understanding and Processing Emotions

48. Unacknowledged: How Negative Emotions Affect Your Mental Health?

49. Unapologetic: Taking Control of Your Mind for a Happier and Healthier Life

50. Uncommon: Transcending the Lies of the Mental Health Industry

51. Unlocked: How to Get Answers from Your Subconscious Mind and Control Your Life

52. Your Full Potential: How to Overcome Fear and Solve Any Problem

53. Your Soul Purpose: Reincarnation and the Spectrum of Consciousness in Human Evolution

About the Publisher

This book was published by 22 Lions Publishing.

www.22Lions.com

www.ingramcontent.com/pod-product-compliance
Lightning Source LLC
LaVergne TN
LVHW022104200926
848481LV00003B/1057
* 9 7 9 8 3 3 0 4 4 7 8 3 1 *